Renee Emerson's ambitio … *Church Ladies*, reads like a … inspiring women from the ages, in particular, Christian "women / growing wild as if sprung up from the dust, / or taken, gently, from a bone." On these poignant pages, we readers discover the kind of unceasing prayer warriors and quirky Sunday School teachers we may have encountered in our youths, or perhaps, rub shoulders with now, who, like the poet writes of Anne Hutchinson, have gone "into the world / bearing no arms, only God's truth." This sensibly orchestrated collection's rich, diverse voices explore the "terrible / separation" between word and deed, man and woman, God and saint. And so we find Susanna Wesley "pray[ing] in her apron tabernacle"; Mary McLeod Bethune, wide-eyed and wise as a serpent, teaching students as the KKK's "cross / screamed *fire* from the front lawn"; and Pandita Ramaba wishing she'd been a mystic but refusing to "pray to be born / exactly what she was not." Indeed, Emerson "swaddle[s]" her readers in the "soft indent / of…ink" as she likewise declares, "If a stone can cry, why / not a woman?" How delighted we are that like Margery Kempe, Emerson, too, has refused to "take up/quietness like a pat of butter on the tongue."

JULIE L. MOORE
author of *Full Worm Moon*

In the poems of *Church Ladies*, Renee Emerson creates vibrant voices for religious women ranging from Saint Hildegard of Bingen to Mahalia Jackson. She complements these memorable monologues with a handful of lyric poems that are prayerful but never preachy; this book would make a splendid gift to yourself or for those you love.

A.M. JUSTER
author of *Wonder and Wrath*

Renee Emerson's *Church Ladies* is an invitation into the lives of women in the church—prophetesses, wives, saints, mothers, martyrs, daughters, and anyone who has been a tender of a family or community: in other words, those who know "the day has no end to its asking." Through lush descriptions, startling images, and a lineage of fierce foremothers, this book illuminates the joys, burdens, steadfastness, and grief of women nurturing faith and the faithful across generations. The faith of Emerson's speakers, however, is not an easy one, nor is it sustained by miracles and majesty. Instead, it's carved out of dailiness and acknowledges the toll of life's losses. In the end, *Church Ladies* is a complex and moving praise song to the persistence of anyone who can say, "when I held out my open hand / I didn't choose what God took from it," and who—like the women of this book—holds out their open hand again and again anyway.

MOLLY SPENCER
author of *If the House* and *Hinge*

From Julian of Norwich to Anne Hutchinson, Mother Teresa, Ruth Graham, and the devoted "church ladies" who pick up small-town kids in their Baptist outreach vans, women are the "roots of spirit sinking down" into the hard soil of church history. With compassion and wit, Emerson illuminates the depths of their devotion, doubt, secrecy, and sacrifice in a way that makes me proud to follow in these flawed and faithful footsteps.

TANIA RUNYAN
author of *What Will Soon Take Place*

Church Ladies

Renee Emerson

Fernwood
PRESS

Church Ladies

©2023 by Renee Emerson

Fernwood Press
Newberg, Oregon
www.fernwoodpress.com

Printed in the United States of America

Cover and page design: Mareesa Fawver Moss

Cover photo: Brett Jordan via Unsplash

ISBN 978-1-59498-104-3

To all the church ladies.
May I too cease to do evil and learn to do good.

Contents

Greeters

We Stay Inside When It Is Storming

My mother always took us out in the rain,
sky large and ominous as a history
selected by men who've never heard
of our town. Lightning, a password
into a natural fury, my mother
did not hold us in the wind, though
some of us were young enough
to straddle her hip, hands in her hair.

A Bradford pear we climbed
every afternoon that summer, when
the air pressed in on the lungs,
and our skin was damp with
morning, broke at the trunk,
knocked teeth out from the privacy fence
between our house and the house of strangers.
The force blew the door open, an invitation.

Our shirts wet and clinging like a stain,
our hair curling in youth and water,
each storm was a sermon; we sat quietly in it,
forbidden from fidgeting. All I remember
is how she never looked at any of us.
All I remember is how she looked up.

Dorothy Sayers, Mystery Writer

In the beginning, there was a loaded tree,
two bodies, romantic intrigue, and a God.
Obedience is the catalyst. Satan
is the villain, but we are the whodunnit,
playing like orphan children in a garden.

It is true that all good stories involve orphans,
the early abandoned. We love their lack
of loneliness, their stalwart adaptability.

My daughters play that the mud is soup,
the tree house a boxcar. They tell me how
they came to be here, little women
growing wild as if sprung up from the dust
or taken, gently, from a bone.

To Martin, on His Wife

Søren Kierkegaard once said Martin Luther
might as well have married a "wooden plank."

Katherine, *Kette*, hidden
in herring barrels, driven
into town to hunt a husband,

of all the renegade nuns, so young,
eyes roving from the cloister,
she refused to be "placed,"
so you wed her.

Doctor Hammer-in-Hand,
she was never a "sexless log,"
six children and a hoard of orphans
clustered in the Black Cloister

homestead. Nowadays, Katie'd be
a keeper—queen of sustainable
living, herbal magician, urban
gardener, butcher, shearer,
nurse, and teacher, she's worth
her weight in backyard chickens,

pecking like the flick of sinner's fire,
the halting promises of reformation,
the ninety-odd things that still need to change.

Firstborn

I straighten and stretch the baby's curled fingers,
watching you climb in the backyard.
It's fenced, but you climb higher than the fence.
Your other sister—the second born, the rival—
is where you want to be. A spider collapses
into a knothole. You tell your sister a lie

so she will be afraid of having what you want.
She's crying now, face red and hair sticking
to her wet cheeks. Now, at the tallest point,
you watch the spider, a connoisseur of height,
approach like tapping fingers, and the baby
is waking up, and your other sisters, there are five,
are forgetting this game. You scream.

Always climbing places where I can't get you down,
I only offer you my thin voice as ladder,
admonishing, needling, and you don't trust it.
We all want someone to climb for us, to lift us
down. That rescue, the rescue that requires sacrifice.

Sunday School Teachers

Anne Hutchinson

You have stepped out of your place, have rather been a husband than a wife, and a preacher than a hearer; and a magistrate rather than a subject. —Reverend Hugh Peter of Salem

Not a wife—a Jezebel.
Not a preacher—a witch.
Not quiet—speaking.
Not beneath you, not bending down,
I have stepped out
of my place, I have
removed my black frock
and petticoats and stamped
them in the mud.

Sometimes the preacher gives
us winterberries, growing
under packed snow
for the mittened hand to paw out.

The preacher gives
us blueberries, growing
in thickets for the black-stained
hand and tin pail.
Then magnolia leaves,
glinting waxed and green, with
shocks of white flower between.

Sometimes the preacher gives
stones, and we throw
them into the rivers, into the fields,
at each other.

I took the sermons, teased
them out, laid them flat,
for all the men and women,
gathering in my living room.

What charge can you bring against me?
I go into the world
bearing no arms, only God's truth.

I go into massacre
with my bonnet hanging
down my back,
the sun bleaching
my fine golden hair.

Mary Lyon's School for Women

Tuition was reduced by the students
performing the domestic chores.

I'll swab the mouths of toilets
to learn Latin conjugates;
I'll dab dust from every surface
to learn trigonometry, physics.

Teach me more than piano, sewing,
not to raise my voice
above a murmur,
not to contradict my elders,
not to look a man
straight in the eye.

I will give what I have always given—
clean windows, clean floors,
straight, even stitches.

And for it, this time, you will
set Prometheus' fire
in the kindling of my mind,
and there is no putting out
that hungry blaze.

She'll See Things Before They Happen

—what the midwife said when Mary McLeod Bethune
was born with both eyes open

She saw Black women walking through a door marked "Enter
to learn." When a spider built a web across it, they saved
the multiplication table of her weaving, slipped in through the side.

Turns out everyone wanted a spot on those dirt floors.
She saw no seats saved; each color as good as another.
She saw classes taught from top of a barrel,
students at cardboard boxes writing their names
with their own fingernails. When men in hoods
came, filing by like teeth in a drunk's mouth,
she kept her eyes open, and the girls stood up
in a row for another lesson, while the cross
screamed fire from the front lawn.

In the end, they knew their Latin conjugations;
in the end, they could say the pledge to this country
with their hands over their hearts
in a language the trustees, the men,
wouldn't recognize, not even for half credit.

Susanna Wesley, Homeschool Mom

Cotton apron over her head like she's playing ghost,
Susanna prays for her little ones (near a dozen),
everyday lectures Home Ec and Kitchen Bible Study,
Latin at Lunch, a Timeline of History,
raising boys for the ministry, girls to read.

Even when nurse rolls over on the newborn,
even when hubby hops train to London,
even when townsfolk light up her window with guns,

Susanna Wesley prays in her apron tabernacle,
grease and jam stained, sweet and savory incense
of all that is burnt up, all that
is young, all that is downright holy.

Literary Mama

Our children...need a mother's whole attention. Can I lawfully divide
my attention by literary efforts? —Harriet Beecher Stowe to her
husband Calvin Stowe.

You must be a literary woman. It is so written in the book of fate.
—Calvin Stowe's reply.

Hold ink to their lips. Liken
their toes to commas, bright eyes
to colons, set within parentheses
mouths, wide-open Os when wailing.

Swaddle them in manuscript.
Mold them with the soft indent
of pen, of ink, jet-black as their hair.

Your characters will be their playmates,
your stories their dreams, woven
for them like any toy a mother weaves
from scrap yarn, remnant cloth.

When they taste simile and metaphor,
they will be glad to have a literary mother,
glad for the sweet drip of language
over lips and tongue.

When you feel along their spines,
trace the embossing, their names
and stories, what makes them
yours and mine.

Foster

When I heard they let the baby die in childbirth,
refused a hospital, I cried for the mother, awkward girl
in her jean skirts and ankle-length values,
her husband's, thrust on her
like a borrowed shirt buttoned to the throat.

Another mother, in Kentucky, reports a child dead
one month, another six months later, the third
six months after that. The state is slow; the state gives
too many chances.

Some mothers walk their backyards with a Coors
in one hand and a phone in the other and say,
"She's around here somewhere," gesturing
vaguely to the crowd from the party, men
and women milling around on the crabgrass.
The neighbor's dog's bark sounds like sobbing.

I've been told by a friend to follow my worries
to their worst conclusion. I follow and feel the breath
from their small bodies softly on my open hand,
which has no power to give or take anything from them.

Phoebe Palmer as Sunday School Lady

A Styrofoam cup of animal crackers,
a cup of watered-down juice. She sets
the places in rows, serves them all.

She knows their names: Ezra, Emma,
June. She wipes their noses.

Here she can hold their hands,
tell them stories in her lap.

Here she is mother, sometimes
called that by mistake.

She has painted her face in ash.
Today her own third child has passed.

Overseas

Canals breach the distance
between homes, reflect their order, a patina,
ocher and dun.

Cobbled streets older than Tennessee, than the South
I never left.

In Rome, Georgia,
I learn that I don't have to teach my daughter
how to walk; steps come naturally as she lets go
of one surface, risking it
for what is just out of reach.

It is easy to hold up one life to another
like we held up apples to the rose tint of early morning
in the local orchard last weekend.

Running our hands over
pocked and dimpled skin,
the flawed surfaces,

noting the difference in shade
where sunlight touched its golden
loveliness, where it did not.

Hannah More, the First Sunday School Lady

The only Bible in town props a flower pot
in the deserted parish.

Children are buried without ceremony.
Farmers warn, "Religion will ruin
the economy of harvest, of growth."

Couldn't be content to pile her hair on her head,
a few lemons or lemon flowers to garnish?
Couldn't be content to write script, stay
in town, with ladies and lords who didn't get it?

Hannah gathers up the children first,
then mothers and fathers, teaches them
what makes a life
grow green and strong:

Scripture, sewing, cooking meat
all the way through,

and the roots of spirit sinking down,
sinking down, into the hard, unworked soil.

Choir

Easter Sunday

No one to place the potted lilies
in a semicircle, fragrant
trumpets raised
around the pulpit.

The piano's teeth delicately
still; guitars lean their long necks
into resting stands.

The Word of the Lord
will not return void.

Outside, nails pierce
the parishioner's tires.
Tickets thin as the pages
of the Psalms pass like the plate,
policemen ushering.

The silence of churches
like the silence of a garden
in the early morning.

An angel sitting, unnoticed,
on a discarded stone.

To Fanny Crosby

I leaned my chin into a doctor's hand,
an egg in a cup, an endearing gesture,
as he shone a bright light, and I peered
into the farthest reaches of clinical beige.

My eyes are prone to ripping, I'm told,
and I'm fitted with help. Now I can see
leaves on trees, a T from an E, the details
that pale into the larger forms of not mattering.

You didn't need such vision, Crosby,
my borrowed sight like you borrow your words,
fitted, personalized, from an office of prayer,
face clasped gently by the All Seeing One
that no one living can see.

We Are All Thieves

We have taken the scriptures in words, and know
nothing of them in ourselves. —Margaret Fell

A gospel in the crook
of my arm.

Psalm tucked in my sleeve,
I've lifted

windows and broken
latches for Esther, Ruth, Jeremiah.

A long coat to cover
the epistles.

Book of Wisdom beneath the tongue.
Leviticus behind the ear.

Cut open my shoes
for Revelation and Jude.

Tucked in my bra:
a minor prophet.

The words of Jesus glint red
up from the bottom of
my purse, tag-clipped off
with my teeth.

No one will miss this
prophecy.

No one will miss this
lament.

Mahalia Jackson

Gospel is everything
I sing, and everything I
sing is gospel,
but that don't mean I got
to live it. Tell my piano player
to get her own hundred
dollars, mine's staying pinned
to my bra, a pretty
safe place. That is gospel.

And this: being a woman
who sings loudest
in the church, and by loudest
I mean best.
You can still hear me
down the block, holy or near it.
The block, its own
kind of gospel, and the church,
both that one and every one,
their own gospels singing gospels
out of each and every throat.

This is the gospel truth:
I'm still just that kid
picking up sticks
on the riverbank,
and the river ain't the Jordan,
and any wings I see don't belong
to angels and sure as hell don't
belong to me.

Song of a Traveling Preacher Woman

Jonah ran the other way
but not Jareena Lee.

She stood in the pew to save
the preacher's piety.

She let the sermon roll a river
off her tongue, a spirit wave;

she poured out the word of God
on every head to save.

If a stone can cry, why
not a woman, why
not a woman as immovable,
as indestructible, as stone?

I Come

For Charlotte Elliot

No one wants to come
just as they are
to the Lord. Only children,
go just as they are to anything—
rumpled hair at the wedding,
shoes on the wrong feet at Grandma's,
too young to have learned better,
to carry a disapproving sneer
to their closets and mirrors.

We come to the altar
with bloodied knees and hands.
We come to the Lord praying,
"Just as I am."

And maybe, yes, it is possible
to cleanse us fools along with the wise.

Flannery O'Connor After Readings

Back to the chickens that don't know I write.

They know feed and scratch,
and we both know peck
and a bit about Mississippi dirt,
the order of things, the pecking order,
not to misalign any feathers.

Anything you need to know,
you can learn from a barnyard;
it's where I've learned what I write,
what makes New York and Boston
uncomfortable at dinner parties, stuffed
on couches eating crackers, listening
to the parts of redemption
they don't understand

what the chickens know. What the hell,
I write it like I see it, as a misfit, a Catholic
lady with an Old Testament outlook on joy.

Song for a Convert

Because I was raised
Southern Baptist, free
from the tongue-click
of catechism and litany,

bound to potluck dinners
and don't get caught
drinkin', I never learned
the proper names for sin.

You claim you can catch me up;
OK, new Adam, here is every
fur and feathered thing—

Duplicity: a few words
father forgot to tell mother.

Vaingloriousness: the song
you sing yourself.

Avarice: a hunger.
Loathing: as good
as murder, and Lust
was only for one of us
to avoid.

Slander: arson of our
house of playing cards.

Wrath: always followed
by "of God."

Sloth: a last animal,
suspended so long
between heaven and earth,
the quicker growing green

negates the creature's need
to cover its own
complete, and shameless,
nakedness.

Counting the Tithes
and Offerings

Lottie Moon

We need to make friends before
we can hope to make converts.

It turns out friends
like to eat. So, I divide
my portions by half
and by half, sending home
what I call "excess"
with the youngest first.

Everyone here is starving.
I become as small
as the children, weightless
and slow; they cling to me
still, though I give them
nothing, not even warmth.

I sign off my last dollar
to this mission.

Where are you, Baptist women?
Do you hold your purses
so close to your hearts?
I'm holding the bone and bloat
of an orphan next to mine,
with a mouth that can't clasp shut.

Hand to hand, let's pass this
empty plate. Let's fill it.

Mary Muller

Once, the milk truck broke
down to give the orphans milk.
Once, God told a baker to bring us
a dozen loaves, golden and crisp,
from the oven.

I knew life with George
would be a life spent praying
for pennies, for bread, for our son
to escape the dead.

Never let anyone know
what we need, but pray,
and God will provide it.

And he does, except sometimes
a little late. So we sell things
and pray harder.

Often, the mail comes just in time.
Often, a brother or sister gives
just as it is needed,

though the money was heavy
in their pockets for months,
as heavy as the amens
on our dry tongues.

Marcella of Rome

She stored her money in the stomachs
of the needy rather than hid it in her purse.

Dollar on a tongue,
a bank in an empty mouth,
coin in a throat, rattle cold
gold in a gizzard,
like children who fill
their bellies with stones
to kill starvation, she gave
her widow wealth to buy
bread. This was her hunger,
and when the foreign armies came
to take what they could,
all they found on her
was her own life, as tattered
and worn as everyone else's.

To Church Ladies Who Marry

It was all you could afford
at the time, bright
gold, woven, diamond
chips. She wears it still
after you forgot to repair
her "real" ring that year
and the next. When she didn't,
she always offered an excuse
before we could notice
her bare hand, thin and free,
the hand I used to study
as it carefully turned
a spoon around a pot, as it
peeled potatoes, husked
corn, as it lifted the broom
head from the floor to beat you
with it. She warned us more
than once not to get a ring
like hers, if we got to choose
one day—the setting too
prominent, it caught on
everything, very often caused
a snag or a rip or a fine cut
on the cheek that took
an age to heal.

Clare of Assisi

Lord help us if we start to think we are good,
that we don't owe God anything. Even before
she sold her fine clothes, cut her gold hair,
only ate every third day, every day kissed
the feet of the poor, she wore a hair shirt
to scrape her skin, keep sin on her mind.
Later she'd tell the sisters, "Our bodies
are not made of stone," so treat them like flesh,
like perishable flesh—as hers twisted and failed,
as it had always failed her and the Lord.

To Church Ladies Who Stretch

Every day she grows stronger, she tells me.
She holds a pose minutes longer
than she ever thought a body who has been
through three deliveries, fifty years of
hard work, and a man who can't recall her
face or his hands on her neck, could hold
a pose so long and straight as if the body
were made of stone broken from a larger
stone, as if the body were as difficult to harm.

To Hildegard

The tenth child, your parents gave you to the church
as tithe; I don't know if I would do the same
had I ten, twenty, a hundred to my name. In our church,
the young families have begun to foster local children,
taken from mothers who are high, forgetful, taken from days
spent strapped in a car seat in the middle of an empty room.

One child has lost all of her words for love, another has lost
the correct shape of his head. He does not know how to hold
himself up, unaccustomed to free movement, to being held.
If Mama shapes up, she'll get them back next month.

You see and hear, *The Lord is holy in anointing*
the dangerously stricken.

Born with a closed fist, I have a blue-collar sensibility
for giving. I count my children as mine. A child asleep
in each bed, innocence nested in every corner of my house,
carefully packed, as if for travel. The day has no end to its asking.

You speak and write, *The Lord is holy in wiping*
the reeking wound.

The Lord, when he spoke to you, Fragile One,
was as *a brilliant light, permeating* your brain;
here all of the lights are out, except for the afternoon
cloud-choked sun, persistent in offering
its white light through drawn shades.

Locks

As I brush my daughter's long hair, Crispina,
I think of your first punishment, to be shaved
of your locks, your twists, your mane.

How thick and rich it must've been,
that snaring river, silken roots, lily's tongue—
the sheen and lure of it, uncovered,
spread beneath the sky and eye—

To have the men think the worst
they could do to you, when you refused
to slit a throat for a god you didn't know,
was cut your braid for the flames,
make public a bald scalp, delicate skin.

Prayer Chain

To Julian of Norwich

I suppose it begins with the wish
    for a moment
alone; then ash
    across a stone floor. You are
entombed with Christ, shut up
    in a room with two
windows like eyes set
    to the past and future,
like mouths open to receive
    mass, forgive the unseen
sins of strangers.

Here we paint rooms white
    before we leave them. Outside
one window, a priest; outside
    the other, a young woman,
wearing the footpath to dirt. Today,
    she carries pears, daisies, certain
testimonies. Tomorrow, she carries her mother.

Isn't this what you prayed for? To burn
    with visions, to suffer like God?
Specter, voice from the living grave,
    are you more pure there
than the maid on the footpath, begging
    penance, shut within
the anchorage
    of an earthly body?

Prayer of Mother Teresa

In my soul I feel just that terrible
pain of loss—of God
not wanting me—of God not being
God—of God not really existing (Jesus
please forgive my blasphemies—
I have been told to write
everything). In my heart
this is not faith—not light—not
trust—there is so much pain—
the pain of longing, the pain of not being
wanted. I want God with all
the powers of my soul—and yet there
between us—there is a terrible
separation.

Unspoken

When your prayer request isn't just
for your grandma's dog, you
quit requesting so much. Don't
request at all, unless asked.
Then it's *How's your mother?*
and you have to decide if you'll
lie in church—*Fine*—or tell
it. She's safe. She's driving down
to Memphis again to check on him,
seems he's got a cyst, dementia,
a severe lack of remorse. Could be worse.
Hard to know the sterile language
of medical. You don't when
you ask God yourself for healing,
for mercy, for deliverance, death.
You ask it like a child; the first
and sometimes only word is *Help*.

Pandita Ramaba

I should've been a mystic.
But my parents knew only
how to worship, never
how to gather food, garden
and tend the ground. We starved,
one after another, until I found myself
in India, married to a common lawyer.
Then after, a widow, refusing
to shave my head
and hope in the salvation
of my dead husband's eternal favor.
I moved to England, I swallowed
up Christianity, trusting in a cross
and savior rather than the caste
and status I was born to. At least
this God did not starve me. At least
this God did not require a woman
to kiss the dirt and pray to be born
exactly what she was not.
I could not believe in that.
I could believe in being chosen.

Alarm

This morning, I stayed in
from my neighborhood walk
in the near-dark of 5:30, my witness
of garages' parting lips, cars slipping out
with headlights gleaming on asphalt.
Always, too, the birdcall,
birdcall, sweet robins and bluebirds,
trilling in the day.

But we live in a neighborhood
with nothing to worry about.
57 percent of men who watch porn would rape
if they wouldn't get caught. A neighborhood
1.5 miles from my in-laws, with children
and elderly, and newlyweds
buying old houses to prime and paint for profit.
The Japanese maples and azaleas splash
blood-colored, prom-dress-vibrant
against brick and siding, like percentages,
like a computer screen and a girl's hair.

My running shoes, always buddied,
sit by the back door, unlaced and open,
brighter pink than I've ever worn before.
When they came in, I was told that,
from a mile away, anyone could spot me,
I wouldn't be missed.

Margery Kempe, to Her Husband, on the Subject of Secret Sin

It wasn't until after the fourteenth birth
that I asked the church to lend a hand.
Sanctioned chastity! Christ
appeared to me in purple silk,
and I never would confess. Husband,
you know what I did. But you can't pretend
not to know me when the visions come
and I roar, casting myself down, eyes full
of the glory of God in our street, our church,
our chamber. Did you expect me to take up
quietness like a pat of butter on the tongue?
Even now, the scribes scratch down my life,
a record of my sainthood, the blessed holiness
of your dearly beloved wife.

Anne Askew's Confession

You have no business with my sin. I won't offer
my handful of lies, fistfuls of lust like a recitation
for teacher, a gift to be opened and savored.

Because you are just a man
with your own pocketful of dirty coins,
your own false teeth, card up the sleeve.
Only a veil between us, here.

I've found that I too can talk to God.
There's no special magic to it, just a willingness
that no instrument of torture or threat or flame
can wring from my body.

Church Hopping

I'm looking for potluck
dinners and little old ladies
who remember most the names
of my children. I'm looking for
a dress code and to be led
in prayer—you tell me
the words, and I'll say them back
to make sure I heard you right.
I want dusty lilies in pots, a podium,
a cross on the wall minus Jesus
because we're Baptist.
Cards with starry-eyed pictures
of missionaries, stacked Styrofoam
cups for coffee.
I can't wait for God's loving hand
to protect us anymore. Have you
ever really been to church
if you haven't made a preacher
mad as hellfire?

Prayer Chain

Upstairs, my children sleeping
in silence wrung from night hours,
the lamplight a cloak, I pray each name,
earnest and fearful, I pray for wars,
their endings and beginnings.

I can ask what I ask.
He will give what he gives.

My neighbor dies of cancer, a gunman
in a synagogue; the trees turn colors slowly
this year; we pay all our bills on time.

A note in the planner next to a chore,
an appointment, prayer becomes both
and neither, pray, pray that life
changes and stays the same, pick it over
like fruit at market, hold the bruises up to God.

St. Teresa of Avila

There is a time for penance, and a time for partridge.

Faith feels like a foot
relinquishing its devotion
to shoes. Nothing left
for your soles but prophecy.

Nothing left to weave
against the cold but visions
of Christ, of demons.

No time to write, take it
in snatches.

A loose thread here, a tuck there.

No roses in your hair, no scent
of magnolia on your wrist.
No bread for the table,
wine and gossip for the lips.

You pick up the vow of poverty,
silence, prayer.

You remove your own name, falling
in ashes to the floor.

Mrs. Smith, Burned for Praying
in Her Own Language

My longing for God is a rustle of paper
in my jacket; held by the elbow,
I'm turned back toward the trial,
where once they spared me only
for being a woman.

I am learning how to watch
a body turn to ash; my children gather
around the hearth to learn the word
of God in a language anyone can speak.

From the pyre, I tell the judge
there is more than one kind of fire.
I tell him I am already burning.

Outreach

Mary Ann Lyth and Mary Calvert

Fourteen women have been brought
to Mbua to be killed and cooked.

So like a man to find a use
for every part of a woman.
They cooked them on the island,
sometimes right in front of missionary huts
to tempt Christian stomachs to growl
a gospel more primal than Bible.
Pyres of smoke tasted the salt air. Canoes
could not row fast enough, shores already
blanketed with the scent of feasting.
The missionary women pled and saved five
from the mouths of their neighbors,
but, as the king said, the dead are dead,
and one way or another, on the final day
we will all be consumed.

Before I Boarded the Train

Corrie ten Boom

I strung up a Bible
between my shoulder blades,
felt its reassuring pat, pat,
our bodies just bodies packed
together in filth, cattled
toward the camp.

My father hid people
behind my bedroom wall
like termites, living encased in wood.
When it was time to be taken, I was
doorjamb, false-front, good-enough,
and strangers survived my sisters.

In the camp, we stood naked
for our medical inspection: a line
of leering soldiers. We slept
end to end, could neither sit up
nor lift our heads to speak, but
we read the Word of the Lord
beneath a bare bulb, translating
scripture into every language,
in every tongue told again
that our flesh is more than flesh.

Until one day an error was made
in my favor: my number on the list
of those to be released, like a ledger,
balanced, with the living and the dead.

Faye Edgerton

—who translated the Bible into the Navajo language

You didn't have a word for fishing, so how could I
explain Peter, the boats of Galilee,
their trembling grasp upon the water?
Men who trapped fish with a hook or a line,
weaving a web of lines. Your people
didn't eat fish and knew little of the sea.
Shepherds you could understand, coaxing
hooved beasts away from thickets, ledges.
Those parables translated best.
So not with a line or a net, but a staff,
I caught the misspellings, the misuse of Christ,
in the hard winters in my trailer
at the edge of a yellow wood,
writing about sin and redemption
in this untranslated language.

Ann Hasseltine Judson's
Letter to Her Parents in America

Your first grandchild was born in the rolling
of a ship at sea, and, born dead, was given
to the sea, a water creature of salt and the deep.

I gave myself to Burma
even more than Adoniram.
To the straw huts, and children,
cigars jutting from their mouths,
to the lepers, skin peeling like paper,
to women I doused in muddy water,
brought up again into a new life
that looked so much like the last.

Your second grandchild was born in the hut,
beneath the Buddhist statues, beside the slow flowing
river. He lived eight months, long enough
for me to believe something
in this life is lasting.

At the end, my hair shaven,
husband in prison, my third-born
daughter sailing steadily toward
death, our North Star.

I still think it worthwhile
to speak the word of God
in a new tongue, though
it burns like holy fire.

Baptized

Rain came fast last night, filling
the backyard like a dirty tub;
the creek crept over its banks,
beneath the slat-wood fence.

The girls screamed to see
their daddy wade out
into the night, to see him
bright-lit with lightning flash,
scooping the old wailing tabby
from the corner of the yard,
where people who lived here before us
chained their dog in every weather.

I sorted clean laundry collapsed
on the floor like a tangle of wildflowers,
domestic concerns flooding over
everyday danger.

In the morning, the water had swept away
detriments, sticks, and shamble.
A neighbor's new sod twisted up
in patches, skin peeling
under sun, earthworms writhing to safety.

The pavement of our suburb frosted
with pebble and mud, slicked up
from the drainage ditch, open-belly of creek.
Furrows where the water receded,
taking with it what it could.

What storms and floods in us
has left the same markings,
rivulets, the same dissembling
of what we so carefully rooted.

Laura Ingalls in My Prairie Town

She keeps her eye on the mud, the bruised
earth, a bite of terrain, the pavement
furrowing the prairie like a throat
choked on a rock. As tough, as mineral
her belief that land returns to itself,
a surprise to everyone to see the soft arms
of a woman against a plow
here, again. On my porch, a purple finch
hugs the feeder, the cool metal hoop
as soft as a branch to the claw.
Feathers martyr the sidewalk.

Revival Widow

After the joy and satisfaction of knowing that I am his by rights—and his forever—I will slip into the background. In short be a lost life. Lost in Bill's. —Ruth Bell Graham

When I was a child, I heard the screaming outside
the gates my medical missionary parents sealed
like a wound—and that was also joy. I wanted
to stay there all my life. Of course,
I met Bill
in college, and he circled
my finger with a ring of no uncertain
terms, unforgiving size.

Once when a fever came, he sent me
to the hospital, left to preach a revival
combing sinners loose from the dusty pews.
The nurse opened the candies he sent me;
I ate each chocolate and caramel
and then had to vomit.

*Like a small death
the closing door
and you through it*
my children only saw the open
Bible and lit bedroom lamp,
my smiling face.
I'd hoped to go to Tibet.
When I held out my open hand,
I didn't choose what God took from it.

Outreach

White van, benevolent budget angel,
circling the rutted road of the trailer park,
a slow, musicless ice-cream call, children
pushed out the door to rest their parents
and TVs. The driver, retired, over eighty,
doesn't get out, digs nails into the wheel,
doesn't honk the horn because she grew up
here, and they expect her. The shuttle
to Children's Church at First Baptist
Hickory Withe, all boys, kindergarten on up
to the age of caring for cookies and Kool-Aid.

You've got to get them young, get them familiar,
moored to pews and fluent in Sunday School tongue,
the breath-weight of scripture pages beneath the thumb.
A plate to take and eat, a plate to pass, and that long walk
down the aisle to say the prayer, every church lady proud
she brought you there.

Therese of Lisieux

... a priest, an apostle, a martyr, a doctor of the church ...
martyrdom was the dream of my youth.

She traced her name in a book held by angels;
she saw her monogram outlined in constellations.

When her mother died to the burning
of breast cancer, a coffin leaned
outside the door. Joe Camel, Joe Cool,
at an angle like an ex-boyfriend or a drunk
brother, indifferent as the empty days
of the following funeral week.

Faith rested its head on her shoulder,
sunk her childhood in piety.

At fifteen, she stalked down a church aisle,
wrapped in swan's down, to shave her head
to the scalp, take a nun's vows.

She wanted a tinderbox and a lit match,
to be cuffed to a campfire with hymns
on her lips. When she found her
"little way," it was love

in the ordinary. For the scattering of feed
to blank-eyed chickens, for the scrubbed
stain in the wash, for peeling potatoes
precisely, knife running over their imperfect
curves, God-ordained blemishes.

To Church Ladies Who Persist

We filled that hole in the garden
big as my arm is thick, though we knew
a living creature burrowed there—
some groundhog, luckless rabbit.
Slept, ate, perhaps bore young. With their plump
hands and dark-lined fingernails, my daughters
helped me claw it closed. Each stamped the turned
ground with a bare foot. Some left to climb maples,
some stayed, resting confident on my hip.
Creatures ourselves, we covered it just to see
if come morning, she'd dig her way out.

Dorothy Day

The world is a smear
of black and white. What more to report?
I'm more "Help Wanted" than "Headline."
Most Catholics want a little more
separation; I'm new at it, I bring them in,
my undeserving poor. Homeless, drug-riddled,
we share sink and yard and kitchen table.
Some keep their nails chewed to the fleshy tips,
but some let them grow long, jagged, and torn.
In this way, they remind me of children. We don't fix them
but give them tools of repair: the Holy Bible, soap, clippers
to be sure. Sometimes they can hardly stand,
so we sell our papers early. My hope is for a colony:
every street a crop, every street corner dizzy with harvest.

Acknowledgments

Thank you to the following journals who have included some of these poems in their pages: 236, 2River Review, Altarwork, Apple Valley Review, Atticus, Burnt Pine, The Chimes, Cumberland River Review, Dappled Things, Earth and Altar, Fathom Magazine, Gravel, I-70 Review, Perspectives Journal, Reformed Journal, St. Austin Review, Saint Katherine Review, Thimblelit, Valley Voices, Windhover, Wizards in Space.

Many of these poems are indebted to the research and inspiration provided from the book 50 Women Every Christian Should Know: Learning from Heroines of the Faith by Michelle DeRusha. However, while based on true events and quotations, these poems should be considered more poetically than historically factual.

I am whole-heartedly grateful for my husband Bryan Emerson for his steady support and encouragement of my work. I am grateful too for my children—Zuzu, June, Wendy, Diana, and Barnabas—who, through their existence, make my work all the more worthwhile.

Title Index

First Line Index

CPSIA information can be obtained
at www.ICGtesting.com
Printed in the USA
JSHW030340260523
42153JS00004B/37